21st Century
Basic Skills
Library

PATTERNS
AT SCHOOL

by Rebecca Felix

Cherry Lake Publishing • Ann Arbor, Michigan

2

Published in the United States of America
by Cherry Lake Publishing
Ann Arbor, Michigan
www.cherrylakepublishing.com

Consultants: Janice A. Bradley, PhD; Marla Conn, ReadAbility, Inc.

Editorial direction and book production: Red Line Editorial

Photo Credits: Kraevski Vitaly/Shutterstock Images, cover, 1; iStockphoto, 4; Rob Marmion/Shutterstock Images, 6; Don Bendickson/Shutterstock Images, 8; iStock/Thinkstock, 10, 16, 18; Polka Dot/Thinkstock, 12; Remus Moise/Shutterstock Images, 14; GlobalStock/iStockphoto, 20

Library of Congress Cataloging-in-Publication Data
Felix, Rebecca, 1984-
  Patterns at school / by Rebecca Felix.
      pages cm. -- (Patterns all around)
  Includes index.
  ISBN 978-1-63188-918-9 (hardcover : alk. paper) -- ISBN 978-1-63188-934-9 (pbk. : alk. paper) -- ISBN 978-1-63188-950-9 (pdf) -- ISBN 978-1-63188-966-0 (hosted ebook)
  1. Pattern perception--Juvenile literature. 2. Shapes--Juvenile literature.
  3. Schools--Juvenile literature. I. Title.

BF294.F45 2015
152.14'23--dc23

2014030000

Cherry Lake Publishing would like to acknowledge the work of The Partnership for 21st Century Skills. Please visit www.p21.org for more information.

Printed in the United States of America
Corporate Graphics Inc.
December 2014

TABLE OF CONTENTS

Patterns

Patterns are all around at school! Patterns are things that **repeat**. These school desks repeat.

Patterns have **cores**. Cores repeat in **order** twice or more.

Here's a school playground pattern! Its core is gray, red.

Art Class

These art class tools show a pattern. Call the pencils A. Call the erasers B. The core is AB.

Letters help show cores. Kole painted a pattern on his hands in art class! Yellow, green, blue is its ABC core.

Tia made a **collage**. Its colors do not repeat in order. They are *not* a pattern.

What's Next?

Ari hops on a pattern at recess! It goes 1 square, 2 squares.

Predict how many squares come next.

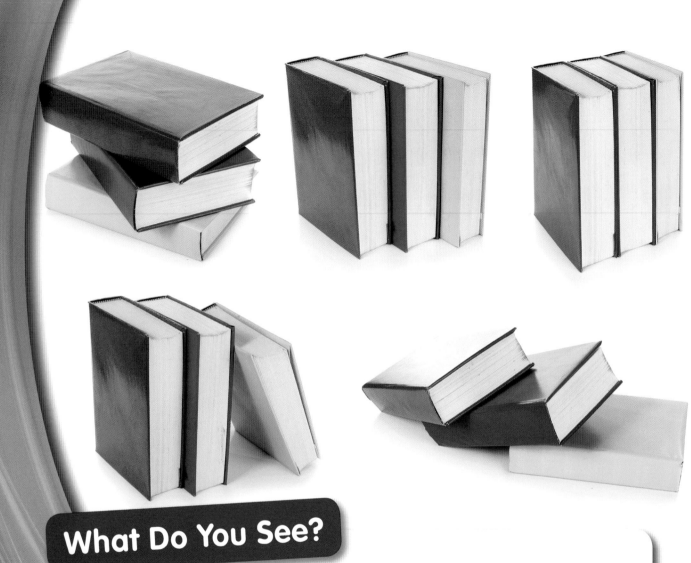

What Do You See?

How many books do you see?

These schoolbooks show a color pattern. What is the core?

What Do You See?

How many rows of beads do you see?

Asa counts beads in math class. The rows show a pattern. Black follows red. What follows yellow?

Find Out More

BOOK

Cleary, Brian P. *A-B-A-B-A: A Book of Pattern Play.*
 Minneapolis, MN: Millbrook Press, 2010.

WEB SITE

Turtlediary.com—Pattern Match
www.turtlediary.com/kindergarten-games/math-games/
pattern-match.html
Play a fun pattern matching game.

Glossary

collage (kuh-LAHJ) art made by gluing things onto a surface

cores (KORZ) the smallest repeating parts of patterns

order (OR-dur) set in a repeating way

predict (pree-DIKT) to say what will come next or in the future

repeat (ri-PEET) to appear or happen again and again

Home and School Connection

Use this list of words from the book to help your child become a better reader. Word games and writing activities can help beginning readers reinforce literacy skills.

all	cores	many	repeat
around	counts	math	rows
art	desks	next	school
beads	erasers	order	schoolbooks
black	follows	painted	show
blue	gray	patterns	square
books	green	pencils	students
call	hands	playground	tools
class	hops	predict	twice
collage	letters	recess	wear
colors	made	red	yellow

What Do You See?

What Do You See? is a feature paired with select photos in this book. It encourages young readers to interact with visual images in order to build the ability to integrate content in various media formats.

You can help your child further evaluate photos in this book with additional activities. Look at the images in the book without the What Do You See? feature. Ask your child to describe one detail in each image, such as a color, activity, or setting.

Index

About the Author

Rebecca Felix is a writer and editor from Saint Paul, Minnesota. She went to school near there while growing up. She loved to draw and color patterns in art class!